Riddles,
JOKES,
Giggles,
Rhymes

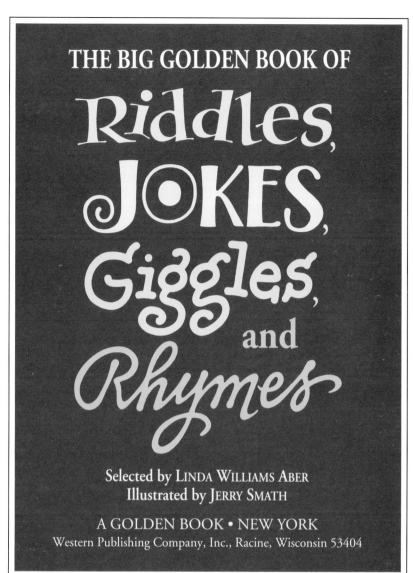

THE BIG GOLDEN BOOK OF
Riddles, JOKES, Giggles, and Rhymes

Selected by LINDA WILLIAMS ABER
Illustrated by JERRY SMATH

A GOLDEN BOOK • NEW YORK
Western Publishing Company, Inc., Racine, Wisconsin 53404

5456793

For Corey and Kip
L.W.A.

To my brother Jim Smath, my favorite comic
J.S.

ACKNOWLEDGMENTS

The editor and publisher have made every effort to trace the ownership of all copyrighted material and to secure permission from copyright holders. Any errors or omissions are inadvertent, and the publisher will be pleased to make the necessary corrections in future printings. Thanks to the following authors, publishers, and agents for permission to use the material indicated:

Linda Williams Aber for "On the Loose With Mother Goose." By permission of the author.

Andre Deutsch Ltd for "The Rhinoceros," "The Ostrich," "The Canary," "The Camel," and "The Porcupine," from *Custard and Company* and *I Wouldn't Have Missed It* by Ogden Nash.

HarperCollins Publishers for "The Green Ribbon" from *In a Dark, Dark Room and Other Scary Stories* by Alvin Schwartz. Text copyright © 1984 by Alvin Schwartz. Reprinted by permission of HarperCollins Publishers.

HarperCollins Publishers for "I Woke Up this Morning" from *Dogs & Dragons, Trees & Dreams* by Karla Kuskin. Copyright © 1980 by Karla Kuskin.

Reprinted by permission of HarperCollins Publishers.

Houghton Mifflin Company for "The Baseball Player" and "At the Beach" from *Doodle Soup* by John Ciardi. Copyright © 1985 by Myra J. Ciardi. Reprinted by permission of Houghton Mifflin Company. All rights reserved.

Little, Brown and Company for "The Rhinoceros," "The Canary," and "The Porcupine" from *Verses From 1929 On* by Ogden Nash. Copyright 1933, 1940, 1942, 1944 by Ogden Nash. "The Canary" and "The Porcupine" first appeared in *The Saturday Evening Post.* By permission of Little, Brown and Company.

Little, Brown and Company for "The Camel" from *Verses From 1929 On* by Ogden Nash. Copyright 1933 by Ogden Nash. First appeared in *The Saturday Evening Post.* By permission of Little, Brown and Company.

Little, Brown and Company for "The Ostrich" from *Verses From 1929 On* by Ogden Nash. Copyright © 1956 by Ogden Nash, copyright © renewed 1984 by Frances Nash, Isabel Nash Eberstadt, and Linell Nash Smith. By permission of Little, Brown and Company.

Little, Brown and Company for "Every Time I Climb a Tree" from *One at a Time* by David McCord. Copyright 1952 by David McCord. By permission of Little, Brown and Company.

William Morrow & Company, Inc., for "I Wish My Father Wouldn't Try to Fix Things Anymore" and "My Mother Made a Meat Loaf" from *Something Big Has Been Here* by Jack Prelutsky. Copyright © 1990 by Jack Prelutsky. By permission of Greenwillow Books, a division of William Morrow & Company, Inc.

William Morrow & Company, Inc., for "Prickled Pickles Don't Smile" from *Vacation Time* by Nikki Giovanni. Copyright © 1980 by Nikki Giovanni. By permission of William Morrow & Company, Inc.

Reed International Books for "I Wish My Father Wouldn't Try to Fix Things Anymore" and "My Mother Made a Meat Loaf" from *Something Big Has Been Here* by Jack Prelutsky, published by William Heinemann Ltd.

Robin Warner for "Spinach." By permission of the author.

CONTENTS

INTRODUCTION

If it's laughter you're after, you've come to the right book! **The Big Golden Book of Riddles, Jokes, Giggles, and Rhymes** *packs a powerful round of punch lines onto every page. Sample this selection of guaranteed giggle-getters, and you'll see right away that it's more than just an ordinary joke book—it's a rib-tickling, knee-slapping, funnybone-busting batch of riddles, limericks, jokes, and rhymes. From the opening Knock, Knocks to the Famous Last Words, you'll find pun-filled fun page after page. Hold on to your sides and get set to laugh out loud.* **The Big Golden Book of Riddles, Jokes, Giggles, and Rhymes** *is about to begin!*

KNOCK, KNOCK. WHO'S THERE?

Knock, knock.
Who's there?
Come in.
Come in who?
Come in, YOU, and read
all the jokes!

Knock, knock.
Who's there?
Wooden shoe.
Wooden shoe who?
Wooden shoe like to sit
down while you read?

Knock, knock.
Who's there?
Midas.
Midas who?
Midas well get comfortable, there
are a lot of these knock, knocks!

Knock, knock.
Who's there?
Ida.
Ida who?
Ida come over sooner if I'd
known there was a party!

Knock, knock.
Who's there?
Radio.
Radio who?
Radio not, here I come!

Knock, knock.
Who's there?
Lettuce.
Lettuce who?
Lettuce come in and visit awhile.

Knock, knock.
Who's there?
Sherwood.
Sherwood who?
Sherwood like to come in.

Knock, knock.
Who's there?
Amish.
Amish who?
Amish you very much.

Knock, knock.
Who's there?
Butter.
Butter who?
Butter hurry up. I can't wait all day!

Knock, knock.
Who's there?
Justin.
Justin who?
Justin time to say goodbye!

TONGUE TANGLERS

Try to say these twisted phrases three times in a row without tangling up your tongue!

☞ Black bug's blood.

☞ A box of biscuits, a box of mixed biscuits, and a biscuit mixer.

☞ He ran from the Andes to the Indies in his undies.

☞ Rubber baby buggy bumpers.

☞ A noisy noise annoys an oyster.

☞ The sixth sheik's sixth sheep's sick.

☞ Some shun sunshine.

☞ This is a zither.

☞ The skunk sat on a stump and thunk the stump stunk. But the stump thunk the skunk stunk.

☞ How much wood would a woodchuck chuck,
If a woodchuck could chuck wood?
He would chuck, he would, as much as he could,
If a woodchuck could chuck wood.

WHAT DO YOU GET . . . ?

If you don't know the answers, turn the page to find out!

1. What do you get when you cross a rooster with a duck?

2. What do you get when you cross an elephant with a penguin?

3. What do you get when you cross a goose with a bull?

4. What do you get when you cross a kangaroo with a chicken?

5. What do you get when you cross a lawn mower with a bird?

6. What do you get when you cross a rabbit with a spider?

7. What do you get when you cross a rooster with a giraffe?

8. What do you get when you cross a parrot with a woodpecker?

9. What do you get when you cross a turkey with a centipede?

10. What do you get when you cross an elephant with a kangaroo?

HERE'S WHAT YOU GET!

If you don't know the riddles, see page 9.

If you don't know the riddles, see page 9.

1. An animal that wakes you up at the quack of dawn.

2. An animal in a very tight-fitting tuxedo.

3. An animal that honks before it runs you over.

4. Pouched eggs.

5. Shredded tweet.

6. A hair net.

7. An animal that can wake up people who live on the top floor of an apartment building.

8. An animal that talks in Morse code.

9. Drumsticks for everyone!

10. Big footprints all over Australia.

DON'T JUDGE A BOOK BY ITS COVER

You won't find these books in any library. Read the titles and authors' names out loud and you'll see why.

EMERGENCY by Colleen Allcars

Fitness FOR EVERYone by STAN DUPP, SID DOWN, and BEN DOVER

OVER THE CLIFF by Hugo First

MY LIFE IN THE CIRCUS BY ELLA FUNT

The Care and Feeding of your PET PARROT by Polly Wanda Craquer

THE JOYS OF ACNE by LOTTA ZITTS

UNDERSTANDING MATH by CAL Q. LATER

UNDER THE SEA by SANDY BOTTOMS

GUIDE TO PUBLIC SPEAKING by MIKE ROFONE

THE PERILS OF POISON IVY by Shirley U. Itch

HOW TO WASH YOUR HAIR by Dan Druff

"GOOD NEWS, BAD NEWS" JOKES

Billy arrived home from school, threw his bag and jacket in a heap on the floor, and went to the kitchen for a snack. His mother greeted him, saying, "Billy, I have some good news and some bad news. The good news is you will never ever have to clean your room again. The bad news is we've rented your room to your Uncle Marvin!"

Sam asked his best friend to find out what the most popular girl in the school thought of him. His friend came back and said, "Sam, I have some good news and some bad news. The good news is she says you remind her of a famous movie star. The bad news is the star you remind her of is King Kong!"

As Mrs. Higgle was leaving for vacation, she asked her neighbor to have her little boy feed her collection of rare tropical fish while she was away. When Mrs. Higgle came back, she asked her neighbor how the feeding had gone. The neighbor said, "I have some good news and some bad news. The good news is he fed all your fish. The bad news is he fed them to the cat!"

When Jill came home from a big ice-skating competition, her best friend asked how she had done in the skating events. "Well," said Jill, "I have some good news and some bad news. The good news is I took the first-place trophy! The bad news is they caught me with it and I had to give it back!"

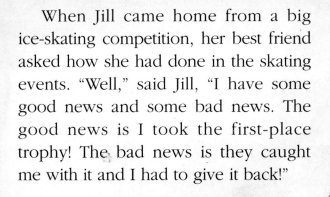

HAVE YOU HEARD
THE ONE ABOUT . . . ?

Have you heard the one about
the three holes in the ground?
Well, well, well.

Have you heard the one about
the jump rope?
Skip it.

Have you heard the one about
dynamite?
It's a blast.

Have you heard the one about
the broken drum?
You can't beat it.

Have you heard the one about
the rubber band?
It's really stretching it.

Have you heard the one about
the fire?
It's hot.

Have you heard the one about
the flu?
It's really sick.

Have you heard the one about
the jar?
Put a lid on it.

COFFEE
+ DONUT
75¢

GOOD SPORTS LAUGHS

The Baseball Player

—What's the score?
—Two hundred to four.
—It looks like the other team's day.
—Well, you can bet
  We're not through yet:
  We still have an inning to play!

John Ciardi

What's the best way to hold a bat?
By the wings.

PROUD FATHER: My boy's been playing ball since he was eight months old.
COACH: Really? He must be awfully tired!

VISITOR: What are you fishing for today?
BOY: Whales.
VISITOR: There are no whales in that pond.
BOY: There isn't anything else, either, so I might as well fish for whales.

COREY: I know everything there is to know about tennis.
KIP: Okay—how many holes are there in a tennis net?

AMATEUR BOXER: Did I do any damage?
COACH: No, but keep swinging your fists, and the draft you create might give him a cold!

What's the quietest sport in the world?
Bowling. You can hear a pin drop.

15

A ZOO FULL OF RHYMES

When it comes to outrageous rhymes, Ogden Nash was one of America's most popular poets. Here are some of the rhymes he made—and some of the silly words he made up!

The Rhinoceros

The rhino is a homely beast,
For human eyes he's not a feast.
Farewell, farewell, you old rhinoceros,
I'll stare at something less prepoceros.

The Ostrich

The ostrich roams the great Sahara.
Its mouth is wide, its neck is narra.
It has such long and lofty legs,
I'm glad it sits to lay its eggs.

The Canary

The song of canaries
Never varies,
And when they're molting
They're pretty revolting.

The Camel

The camel has a single hump;
The dromedary, two;
Or else the other way around.
I'm never sure. Are you?

The Porcupine

Any hound a porcupine nudges
Can't be blamed for harboring grudges.
I know one hound that laughed all winter
At a porcupine that sat on a splinter.

Ogden Nash

17

SERVICE WITH A LAUGH

Waiter, this fish isn't as good as the fish I had last week.
That's strange, sir. It's the same fish!

How did you find the meat, Madame?
I just looked under the potato chip and there it was!

Waiter, what's this fly doing in my soup?
I think it's the backstroke, sir.

Waiter, there's a dead fly in my soup.
I know, sir. It's the heat that kills them.

Waiter, this food isn't fit for a pig.
I'm sorry, sir. I'll bring you some that is.

Waiter, this fish is bad.
You naughty fish, you!

LUNCH COUNTER LINGO

If you live in or visit a town with a lunch counter, you may notice that short-order cooks, waitresses, and waiters have a language all their own so they can fill orders quickly. Here are some tasty samples of some fast-food fast talk.

What They Say	What They Mean
Adam and Eve on a Raft	two scrambled eggs on toast
Bossy in a Bowl	beef stew
A Bowl	today's soup
Bowl of Red	chili
Bucket of Mud	chocolate ice cream
Crowd	three of anything
Gee-A-Cee and Tommy	grilled cheese with tomato
Grade-A	milk
Hay In	strawberry soda
Let It Walk	take-out order
One In	chocolate ice-cream soda
Pine In	pineapple soda
Red Stretch	Cherry Coke
A Shimmy	Jell-O
A Smear	with butter
Stretch One	Coke
Stretch One and Make It Pucker	Coke with lemon

A GEE-A-CEE and TOMMY WITH ONE IN, A BUCKET OF MUD, and LET IT WALK!

MENU

DEFINITELY DAFFY DEFINITIONS

ajar: what jam comes in

Band-Aid: a fund for needy rock musicians

cross-examination: a test given by an angry teacher

deceit: the back of your pants

female snake: a hiss miss

hogwash: where pigs do their laundry

icicle: a frozen bike

mushroom: where school cafeteria food is kept

Nutcracker Suite: a squirrel's hotel room

paradox: two ducks instead of one

roll call: the sound made by a sesame-seed bun

slacks: lazy pants

tricycle: a tot-rod

wisecracker: a smart cookie

NIFTY TOM SWIFTIES

In the 1920s jokes called Tom Swifties made everyone laugh. Can you see why?

"Yes, I understood immediately," said Tom Swiftly.

"It's a copy machine, it's a copy machine," said Tom repeatedly.

"I'll never pet a lion again," said Tom offhandedly.

"I wasn't in school today," said Tom absently.

"I broke my pencil tip," said Tom pointlessly.

"It's like a fairy tale," Tom said grimly.

"I dropped the toothpaste," said Tom, crestfallen.

"Stop the horse!" said Tom woefully.

"Everyone loses a few games," said Tom winsomely.

"You're one in a thousand," said Tom grandly.

"I haven't a clue," said Tom thoughtlessly.

"I could go on like this forever," said Tom endlessly.

I WISH MY FATHER WOULDN'T TRY TO FIX THINGS ANYMORE

My father's listed everything
he's planning to repair,
I hope he won't attempt it,
for the talent isn't there,
he tinkered with the toaster
when the toaster wouldn't pop,
now we keep it disconnected,
but we cannot make it stop.

He fiddled with the blender,
and he took a clock apart,
the clock is running backward,
and the blender will not start,
every windowpane he's puttied
now admits the slightest breeze,
and he's half destroyed the furnace,
if we're lucky, we won't freeze.

The TV set was working,
yet he thought he'd poke around,
now the picture's out of focus,
and there isn't any sound,
there's a faucet in the basement
that had dripped one drop all year,
since he fixed it, we can't find it
without wearing scuba gear.

I wish my father wouldn't try
to fix things anymore,
for everything he's mended
is more broken than before,
if my father finally fixes
every item on his list,
we'll be living in the garden,
for our house will not exist.

Jack Prelutsky

23

CLASS LAUGHS FROM
THE SCHOOL OF HUMOR

TEACHER: Skip, can you give me a sentence using the word *miniature*?
SKIP: Sure. You start snoring the miniature asleep.

TEACHER: This essay on your pet cat is word for word the same as your sister's.
JENNY: It's the same cat.

CHRIS: I didn't deserve a zero on this paper!
TEACHER: No, but there weren't any lower marks.

TEACHER: Where is your pencil, Mark?
MARK: I ain't got one.
TEACHER: How many times have I told you not to say that, Mark? Now, listen. *I do not have* a pencil, *you do not have* a pencil, *they do not have* a pencil. Now do you understand?
MARK: Not really. What happened to all the pencils?

TEACHER: I asked you to write an essay on cheese last night. Where is it?
MATT: I tried, but the cheese kept blocking up the tip of my pen!

TEACHER: You look pretty dirty, Lia.
LIA: I'm even prettier when I'm clean!

TEACHER: What happened to your homework?
STEVE: I made it into a paper airplane and somebody hijacked it.

TEACHER: What's a Grecian urn?
MIKE: About $300 a week.

TEACHER: Can you tell me something that didn't exist 100 years ago?
SARAH: Yes—me!

TEACHER: What are the smaller rivers that make up the Nile called?
ROBBY: Juve-Niles.

LIMERICKS

A diner while dining at Crewe
Found quite a large mouse in his stew.
Said the waiter, "Don't shout
And wave it about,
Or the rest will be wanting one, too."

There was a young lady, a Swiss,
Who said, "I think skating is bliss."
But a change in her fate
Came when her skate
Made her finish up something like this.

26

There was an old man of Nantucket
Who kept all his cash in a bucket,
But his daughter named Nan
Drove away in a van—
And as for the bucket, Nantucket!

A delicate girl named Louise
Caused quite a big stir with her sneeze.
One small twitch of her nose
And folks cried, "Thar she blows!"
She's a whale of a gal, if you please!

27

ALPHABET CHUCKLES

Why is an island like the letter T?
Because it is in the middle of water.

What occurs once in every minute, twice in every moment, but not in a thousand years?
The letter M.

Why is the letter C like a magician?
It turns ash into cash.

What two letters did Old Mother Hubbard find in her cupboard?
MT.

What is in the middle of Paris?
The letter R.

Why is the letter V like an angry bull?
Because it comes after U.

Why is the letter G such a party-pooper?
Because it always ends everything.

PRICKLED PICKLES DON'T SMILE

Never tickle
a prickled pickle
cause prickled pickles
Don't smile

Never goad
a loaded toad
when he has to walk
A whole mile

Froggies go courting
with weather reporting
that indicates
There are no snows

But always remember
the month of December
is very hard
On your nose

Nikki Giovanni

THE GREEN RIBBON

Once there was a girl named Jenny.
She was like all the other girls,
except for one thing.
She always wore a green ribbon
around her neck.
There was a boy named Alfred
in her class.
Alfred liked Jenny,
and Jenny liked Alfred.
One day he asked her,
"Why do you wear that ribbon
all the time?"
"I cannot tell you," said Jenny.
But Alfred kept asking,
"Why *do* you wear it?"
And Jenny would say,
"It is not important."
Jenny and Alfred grew up
and fell in love.
One day they got married.

After their wedding,
Alfred said,
"Now that we are married,
you must tell me
about the green ribbon."
"You still must wait,"
said Jenny.
"I will tell you
when the right time comes."
Years passed.
Alfred and Jenny grew old.
One day Jenny became very sick.
The doctor told her she was dying.
Jenny called Alfred to her side.
"Alfred," she said, "now I can tell you
about the green ribbon.
Untie it, and you will see
why I could not tell you before."
Slowly and carefully,
Alfred untied the ribbon,
and Jenny's head fell off.

Alvin Schwartz

FOOLISH, GHOULISH MONSTER JOKES

Why do vampires make good friends?
They'll always go to bat for you.

What happened when the vampire started writing poetry?
Things went from bat to verse.

What do you call a dentist who offers to clean a werewolf's teeth?
Crazy.

Why did the young ghoul measure himself against the wall?
He wanted to know if he'd gruesome.

What goes "Ha, ha, ha, plop!"?
A monster laughing his head off.

What is a ghost's favorite dessert?
Boo-berry pie and I scream.

Where did the Wolf Man go to make his first movie?
Howl-lywood.

What did the doctor give Count Dracula for his cold?
Coffin syrup.

What bites but isn't alive?
Frost.

What do monsters eat for breakfast?
Dreaded wheat.

MEDICAL MADNESS

DOCTOR: Nurse, did you take the patient's temperature?
NURSE: No, is it missing?

PATIENT: Doctor, I keep thinking I'm a bridge.
DOCTOR: What's come over you?
PATIENT: Two trucks, three buses, and thirteen cars.

PATIENT: Doctor, I can't seem to remember anything anymore.
DOCTOR: How long have you had this problem?
PATIENT: What problem?

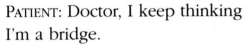

DOCTOR: You need glasses.
PATIENT: How can you tell?
DOCTOR: I knew as soon as you came through the window.

PATIENT: What should I take when I'm run down?
DOCTOR: The license plate number.

PATIENT: Your cure didn't work.
DOCTOR: Did you drink a glass of milk after a hot bath?
PATIENT: No, after drinking the hot bath, I didn't feel like having any milk.

ON THE LOOSE WITH MOTHER GOOSE

Humpty Dumpty

Humpty Dumpty sat on a wall,
Humpty Dumpty had a great fall,
All the king's horses and all the king's men
Said sadly, "Oh, well, scrambled eggs again!"

Old Mother Hubbard

Old Mother Hubbard
Went to the cupboard
To get her poor dog some meat.
The cupboard was bare
With no food to spare—
So she took her dog out to eat!

Mary Had a Little Lamb

Mary had a little lamb,
Its fleece was white as snow,
And everywhere that Mary went
The lamb was sure to go.
She brought the lamb to school one day,
A generous thing to do,
For now the cafeteria
Serves Mary's little lamb stew!

The Old Woman in the Shoe

There was an old woman
Who lived in a shoe,
With the shortage of houses
What else could she do?
She had lots of children
And no room to spare,
So she sold her one shoe
And moved to a pair!

Linda Williams Aber

WHAT DO YOU CALL IT?

What do you call a cat that sucks a lemon?
A sour puss.

What do you call two banana peels?
A pair of slippers.

What do you call a sleeping bull?
A bulldozer.

What do you call the life story of a car?
An auto-biography.

What do you call a woman who goes fishing?
Annette.

What do you call two spiders who have just gotten married?
Newlywebs.

What do you call a man who swims back and forth across the English Channel without taking a bath?
A dirty double-crosser.

WHO EVER SAID
VEGETABLES AREN'T FUNNY?

Spinach

Green, green, ghastly green,
Crawling all over my plate,
Destroying my mashed potatoes,
And now it's almost too late!
It's all over my dish,
Upsetting my fish,
Attacking my seedless rye bread;
Oh, when will it stop,
This green slimy glop?
If I eat it, I'll surely be dead!

Robin Warner

What vegetable is dangerous to have on board a ship?
A leek.

What is a cannibal's favorite vegetable?
Baked beings.

Why should you never tell secrets in a vegetable garden?
*Because the cornstalks have ears, the potatoes have eyes,
and the beans talk.*

THE OLDEST JOKES IN THE WORLD

KATE: What did one flea say to the other flea?
NATE: Should we walk, or do you want to take a dog?

BILL: The police are looking for a man with one eye called Bernie.
PHIL: What's the other eye called?

DAN: Why did Harry tiptoe past the medicine cabinet?
ANN: He didn't want to wake the sleeping pills.

WILL: Would you call me a taxi?
JILL: Okay. You're a taxi.

MOE: Would you make me a milkshake?
JOE: ZAP! You're a milkshake!

SAL: Why did your sister get arrested at the zoo last week?
VAL: She was feeding the pigeons.
SAL: What's wrong with that?
VAL: She was feeding them to the lions!

SAM: Where does King Kong sleep?
PAM: Anywhere he wants to!

JACK: What's black and white and red all over?
ZAK: A newspaper.

DON: What has four wheels and flies?
JOHN: A garbage truck.

STAN: I lost my dog last week.
VAN: Why don't you put an ad in the newspaper?
STAN: It won't do any good. He can't read.

FATHER WILLIAM

From *Alice's Adventures in Wonderland*
By Lewis Carroll

"You are old, Father William," the young man said,
"And your hair has become very white;
And yet you incessantly stand on your head—
Do you think, at your age, it is right?"

"In my youth," Father William replied to his son,
"I feared it might injure the brain;
But, now that I'm perfectly sure I have none,
Why, I do it again and again."

"You are old," said the youth, "as I mentioned before,
And have grown most uncommonly fat;
Yet you turned a back-somersault in at the door—
Pray, what is the reason of that?"

"In my youth," said the sage, as he shook his gray locks,
"I kept all my limbs very supple.
By the use of this ointment—one penny the box—
Allow me to sell you a couple?"

"You are old," said the youth, "and your jaws are too weak
For anything tougher than suet;
Yet you finished the goose, with the bones and the beak—
Pray, how did you manage to do it?"

"In my youth," said his father, "I took to the law,
And argued each case with my wife;
And the muscular strength, which it gave to my jaw,
Has lasted the rest of my life."

"You are old," said the youth, "one would hardly suppose
That your eye was as steady as ever;
Yet you balanced an eel on the end of your nose—
What made you so awfully clever?"

"I have answered three questions, and that is enough,"
Said his father. "Don't give yourself airs!
Do you think I can listen all day to such stuff?
Be off, or I'll kick you downstairs!"

THE BEST (AND WORST!) PICKLE, GRAPE, AND BANANA JOKES

Why doesn't a pickle like to travel?
Because it's a jarring experience!

Why did the pickle climb the ladder to the roof?
He heard the meal was on the house.

What's green, has twenty-two legs, and plays football in cold weather?
The Green Bay Pickles.

What's round, purple, and used to rule the waves?
Grape Britain.

How do you say *grape* in Japanese?
"Grape in Japanese."

When is it all right to eat grapes with fingers?
Never. Grapes don't have fingers.

What attracts one banana to another?
Apeel.

What do two bananas get when they become tired
of being married?
A banana split.

What's soft and yellow and very dangerous?
Shark-infested banana cream pie.

Why don't bananas snore?
They don't want to wake up the rest of the bunch.

FRESH

MY MOTHER MADE A MEAT LOAF

My mother made a meat loaf
that provided much distress,
she tried her best to serve it,
but she met with no success,
her sharpest knife was powerless
to cut a single slice,
and her efforts with a cleaver
failed completely to suffice.

She whacked it with a hammer,
and she smacked it with a brick,
but she couldn't faze that meat loaf,
it remained without a nick,
I decided I would help her
and assailed it with a drill,
but the drill made no impression,
though I worked with all my skill.

We chipped at it with chisels,
but we didn't make a dent,
it appeared my mother's meat loaf
was much harder than cement,
then we set upon that meat loaf
with a hatchet and an ax,
but that meat loaf stayed unblemished
and withstood our fierce attacks.

We borrowed bows and arrows,
and we fired at close range,
it didn't make a difference,
for that meat loaf didn't change,
we beset it with a blowtorch,
but we couldn't find a flaw,
and we both were flabbergasted
when it broke the power saw.

We hired a hippopotamus
to trample it around,
but that meat loaf was so mighty
that it simply stood its ground,
now we manufacture meat loaves
by the millions, all year long,
they are famous in construction,
building houses tall and strong.

Jack Prelutsky

VACATION CHUCKLES

At the Beach

—Johnny, Johnny, let go of that crab!
  You have only ten fingers, you know:
  If you hold it that way, it is certain to grab
  At least one or two of them. Please, let go!

—Thank you, Daddy, for teaching not scolding,
  But there's one thing I think you should know:
  I believe it's the crab that is doing the holding—
  I let go—OUCH!—ten minutes ago!

John Ciardi

BEN: How long will you be on vacation?
KEN: About five feet six inches, same as I am now!

TRACY: Are you taking the train to your aunt's house for your vacation?
STACY: No, it's too heavy.

JOE: My parents said for vacation we're going on a Double Mystery Tour.
MOE: What do you mean?
JOE: Well, we don't know where we're going, and we don't know how we're going to pay for it!

SIGNS OF THE TIMES

There are laughs all around. You just have to look for the signs!

I WOKE UP THIS MORNING

I woke up this morning
At quarter past seven.
I kicked up the covers
And stuck out my toe.
And ever since then
(That's a quarter past seven)
They haven't said anything
Other than "No."
They haven't said anything
Other than "Please, dear,
Don't do what you're doing,"
Or "Lower your voice."
Whatever I've done
And however I've chosen,
I've done the wrong thing
And I've made the wrong choice.
I didn't wash well
And I didn't say thank you.
I didn't shake hands
And I didn't say please.
I didn't say sorry
When passing the candy.
I banged the box into
Miss Witelson's knees.
I didn't say sorry.
I didn't stand straighter.
I didn't speak louder
When asked what I'd said.
Well, I said
That tomorrow
At quarter past seven
They can
Come in and get me.
I'm Staying In Bed.

Karla Kuskin

51

WOODEN YOU LIKE A LAUGH?

Sure, you wood! You don't need a wooden dummy—just a good routine.

VENTRILOQUIST: How was your visit with your cousin?

DUMMY: Bad. Really bad. As soon as I got there, he said I had to make my own bed.

VENTRILOQUIST: Well, that's not too much to ask, is it?

DUMMY: No, except I had to make it with a hammer and saw!

VENTRILOQUIST: I see. But it must have been fun to see the family again.

DUMMY: Not really. My uncle is very sick. He thinks he's a chicken!

VENTRILOQUIST: A chicken! Gee, you should put him in the hospital.

DUMMY: We would have, but we needed the eggs!

VENTRILOQUIST: Well, when are you going back?

DUMMY: Can't.

VENTRILOQUIST: Can't? Why not?

DUMMY: My aunt and uncle are mad at me. When I got there, they said, "Our house is your house."

VENTRILOQUIST: Very nice.

DUMMY: So I sold it!

VENTRILOQUIST: Oh, dear. Well, say "Good night," Dummy.

DUMMY: Good night, Dummy.

WHY? WHY? WHY? RIDDLES

If you don't know the answers, turn the page.

1. Why did the chicken cross the road?

2. Why did the turtle cross the road?

3. Why was the strawberry worried?

4. Why must a robber be strong?

5. Why does a hen lay eggs?

6. Why do lions eat raw meat?

7. Why don't ducks tell jokes while they are flying?

8. Why did the sword-swallower eat pins and needles?

9. What would you think if you found bones on the moon?

WHY? WHY? WHY? ANSWERS

If you don't know the riddles, see page 53.

1. To get away from home. He felt cooped up.

2. To get to the Shell station.

3. Because its mother was in a jam.

4. So he can hold up a bank.

5. Because if she dropped them, they would break.

6. They don't know how to cook.

7. Because they would quack up.

8. He was on a diet.

9. The cow didn't make it.

EVERY TIME I CLIMB A TREE

Every time I climb a tree
Every time I climb a tree
Every time I climb a tree
I scrape a leg
Or skin a knee
And every time I climb a tree
I find some ants
Or dodge a bee
And get the ants
All over me

And every time I climb a tree
Where have you been?
They say to me
But don't they know that I am free
Every time I climb a tree?
I like it best
To spot a nest
That has an egg
Or maybe three
And then I skin
The other leg
But every time I climb a tree
I see a lot of things to see
Swallows rooftops and TV
And all the fields and farms there be
Every time I climb a tree
Though climbing may be good for ants
It isn't awfully good for pants
But still it's pretty good for me
Every time I climb a tree

David McCord

55

SHOPPING FOR LAUGHS

CUSTOMER: Good morning, sir. Can you tell me what's on sale this week?

GROCER: Everything. You didn't think we'd give it away, did you?

CUSTOMER: No, of course not. What I meant was, what's reduced?

GROCER: My wife. She's lost twenty pounds. Looks good. Now, what can I do for you?

CUSTOMER: Do you have any spareribs?

GROCER: Nope, I need every rib I've got.

CUSTOMER: And your liver?

GROCER: Can't live without my liver, lady.

CUSTOMER: Sir, do you always treat your customers like this?

GROCER: Nope, only the special ones. Now, have you made up your mind yet?

CUSTOMER: Well, I think it's going to be another store. I'm not too crazy about your sharp tongue.

GROCER: Tongue? Too sharp? Well, some of the customers think the tongue has a tangy flavor, but you get used to it.

CUSTOMER: Maybe a big salad would be the best thing. Do you have a head of lettuce?

GROCER: Does it look that way? I guess I forgot to comb my hair this morning.

CUSTOMER: Do you carry onions by the pound?

GROCER: Not since I hurt my back. Can't carry anything much anymore. In fact, I feel too weak to even carry on this conversation any longer.

CUSTOMER: Well! I hope your day isn't spoiled!

GROCER: Don't worry, the only thing spoiled here is the meat. Oh, are you leaving so soon?

CUSTOMER: Not soon enough! Good day, sir.

GROCER: Maybe it will be, now that you're leaving!

LIMERICKS AGAIN

A young soccer player from Lyme
Scored a goal for the very first time.
Although he was glad,
His teammates were sad,
He hadn't changed ends at halftime!

There was an old man of Blackheath,
Who sat on his set of false teeth.
Said he with a start,
"O Lord, bless my heart!
I've bitten myself underneath!"

There was a young girl from St. Paul,
Wore a newspaper dress to the ball.
But the dress caught on fire,
And burned her entire,
Front page, sports section, and all.

Cousin Joe dropped by on his way,
And continued to stay and to stay.
Said the host, "When you go,
Please let me know,
And I will return on that day!"

59

RIDDLES IN JEOPARDY

For a change, turn the tables: You give the answer and ask someone to come up with the question.

ANSWER: Engineers.
QUESTION: What kind of ears do engines have?

ANSWER: A cow walking backward.
QUESTION: What goes "Oom! Oom!"?

ANSWER: Retail store.
QUESTION: Where can a dog go to get a new tail, if he loses the one he has?

ANSWER: Foiled again!
QUESTION: What did the leftovers say when they were put into the freezer?

ANSWER: Well, I'll be a monkey's uncle!
QUESTION: What did the monkey say when his sister had a baby?

ANSWER: No, I'm John Smith from the Earth.
QUESTION: Are you tan from the Sun?

ANSWER: Your calves.
QUESTION: What two animals follow you everywhere you go?

KNOCK, KNOCK. BACK AGAIN

Knock, knock.
Who's there?
Olive.
Olive who?
Olive you.

Knock, knock.
Who's there?
Atch.
Atch who?
Gesundheit!

Knock, knock.
Who's there?
Wendy.
Wendy who?
Wendy jokes are over, you'd better laugh!

Knock, knock.
Who's there?
Heart.
Heart who?
Heart to hear you speak, speak louder!

Knock, knock.
Who's there?
Noah.
Noah who?
Noah fence, but these jokes aren't that funny!

HERE COME THE ELEPHANTS!

Why were the elephants the last animals to leave the ark?
Because they had to pack their trunks.

How can you tell if an elephant has been in your refrigerator?
By the footprints in the butter.

Why do elephants wear green nail polish?
So they can hide in a cabbage patch.

Why did the elephant sit on the marshmallow?
To keep from falling in the hot chocolate.

What's the difference between an elephant and a flea?
An elephant can have fleas, but a flea can't have elephants.

Why did the elephant wear sunglasses?
So he wouldn't be recognized when he went out.

Why are elephants wrinkled all over?
Because they're too difficult to iron.

What's the difference between an elephant and a doughnut?
You can't dip an elephant in your coffee.

OUT-OF-THIS-WORLD JOKES

1ST SPACEMAN: How did you break your leg?
2ND SPACEMAN: See those stars over there?
1ST SPACEMAN: Yeah.
2ND SPACEMAN: Well, I didn't.

1ST ASTRONAUT: Do you have any travel tips
for me when I go to the moon?
2ND ASTRONAUT: Yes, take lots of money.
The moon may be down to its last quarter.

What game do spacemen play?
Moon-opoly.

What's an astronaut's favorite food?
Launcheon meat.

Why is football the favorite sport of astronauts?
Because it's played on AstroTurf.

FAMOUS LAST WORDS

Tombstones are the final chance to get in the last word. Some people take good advantage of the space. Here are some famous last words of not-so-famous folks.

MUSIC TEACHER

Stephen and time
Are now both even:
Stephen beat time
Now time's beat
Stephen.

ROBOT
RUST
IN
PEACE

John Yeast
"Pardon me
for not rising"

UNKNOWN PERSON
"I
TOLD YOU
I
WAS SICK"

MARGIE BENT

Here lies the body of
Margie Bent.
She kicked up her
heels and away
she went.

I love you

Love